ANIMAL SCIENCE

**1976 Printing of the
1975 Edition**

BOY SCOUTS OF AMERICA
NORTH BRUNSWICK, NEW JERSEY

Requirements

1. Name four breeds of livestock in each of the following classifications: horses, dairy cattle, beef cattle, sheep, hogs. Tell their principal uses and merits. Tell where the breeds originated.
2. List the principal diseases in your area that afflict the animals in each classification. Describe the symptoms and explain the proper treatment for the diseases you list.
3. Explain the major differences in digestive systems of ruminant and nonruminant animals.
4. Tell how you would properly manage a cow, sheep, horse, or hog, including adequate feeding. Tell what must be done to prevent illness, blemishes, defects, and diseases arising from improper and unsanitary conditions.
5. Tell about career opportunities in livestock production.
6. Complete one of the following options:

Dairying Option

a. Tell how a cow converts forage and grain into milk.
b. Make a chart showing the ingredients in cows' milk. Chart the amount of each.
c. Tell the difference between certified and pasteurized milk. Tell how milk is pasteurized.
d. Tell about the kinds of equipment and health standards for dairy farms.
e. Visit a dairy farm or milk processing plant. Tell about your visit.

Beef Cattle Option

a. Visit a farm or ranch where beef cattle are produced under any of these systems: (1) feeding market cattle for slaughter; (2) producing feeder cattle for sale to commercial cattle feeders; (3) producing purebred cattle for sale as breeding stock to other breeders. Tell how the cattle

Copyright © 1975
Boy Scouts of America
North Brunswick, N.J.
Library of Congress
Catalog Card
Number: 19-600
ISBN 0-8395-3395-0
Printed in the U.S.A.
No. 3395   6M176

were handled, fed, weighed, and shipped.

b. Sketch a plan of a feedlot, hay and grain storage facilities, and loading chute for 30 or more fattening steers, or a corral plan with cutting and loading chutes for handling 50 or more beef cows and their calves at one time.

c. Submit a sketch showing the principal wholesale and retail cuts of beef. Tell about the USDA dual grading system of beef. Tell about the grades in each system.

Hog Option

a. Visit a farm where hog production is a major project, or visit a packing plant or stockyard handling hogs. Describe your visit.

b. Outline in writing the proper feeding from the breeding of gilt or sow through the weaning of the litter. Discuss the growth and finishing periods.

c. Make a sketch showing the principal wholesale and retail cuts of pork. Tell about the recommended USDA grades of pork. Tell the basis for each grade.

Horse Option

a. Make a sketch of a useful saddle-horse barn and exercise yard.

b. Tell the history of the horse and the benefits it has brought to man.

c. Tell about the following terms: mustang, quarter horse, pinto, draft, gelding, calico, palomino,

pacer, trotter, filly, mare, stallion, colt, and foal.

d. Visit a horse farm. Describe your visit.

Poultry Option

a. Keep management records on a brood of 20 chicks (sexed or straight run) for 5 months. Record feed consumption, medication, mortality, and vaccination. Present the records for review.

b. Do *one:*
(1) Manage an egg-producing flock for 5 months. Keep records of feed purchased, eggs sold, and mortality. Present records for review. Tell about the grading of eggs.
(2) Raise 20 chicks, poults, or ducklings. Keep records of feed intake and weight gains. Present records for review. Kill and dress two birds. Tell about grades of poultry.

Sheep Option

a. Make a sketch of a live lamb. Show the location of the various wholesale and retail cuts.

b. Make and exhibit and explain four blood grades (American) of wool. Tell how wool is processed from shearing to the finished product.

c. Visit a farm or ranch where sheep are raised. Tell about your visit, including the feeding program used.

d. Describe some differences between the production of native lambs and the production of range lambs.

Contents

Livestock Breeds

A horse is a horse, right? A cow is a cow and a sheep is a sheep. Well, yes. But a Scout who has grown up with livestock, or even pets, knows that there's more to it than that.

A Thoroughbred and a draft horse are both horses, but they are bred for different purposes—one for speed and the other for strength. And a cow may be a milker or a beef animal. Furthermore, if it is a milk cow, it may be from a breed that produces great quantities of milk with fairly low butterfat, or less milk with high butterfat content.

The same principle of breed differences holds true for other livestock. And so it is important for a livestock producer to know the advantages and drawbacks of various breeds.

But it is also important for the producer to know that there may be greater differences *within* a single breed than between breeds. For example, on the average, a Holstein cow will give more milk than a Jersey. But a healthy, well-tended Jersey whose sire and dam were superior animals may be a bigger milk producer than an unthrifty Holstein whose parents had inferior records.

For this reason, a livestock producer is constantly trying to upgrade his herd or flock. He breeds or buys animals that will improve the herd's production. And, of course, he pays the closest attention to the condition of his stock, making sure that all animals are healthy and have the minimum requirements for feed, shelter, and sanitation. These measures—good breeding and good maintenance—are the route to success in livestock production.

Many breeds of the various kinds of livestock are produced in the United States. In this chapter we will discuss a few of the principal breeds of horses, dairy cattle, beef cattle, sheep, and hogs. If you are interested in a breed that is not covered, look in the literature for the animal in the chapter called "Resources for Your Specialty." Or ask your merit badge counselor or county agent where you can get more information.

Horses

In 1920, about the time your grandfather was a boy, there were 27 million horses in our country. By 1960 there were only a little over 3 million. The big drop was caused by the internal combustion engine.

Horses did most of the heavy farm hauling in 1920 and were also still in use for transportation by buggy. Today the tractor, the truck, and the automobile do the work of hauling and transporting people.

But don't count the horse out! In recent years the horse population has been growing very fast. Today there are somewhere between 7 million and 10 million horses in the United States. The main reason for the comeback of the horse is the booming popularity of riding and racing and the increase in leisure time to enjoy them.

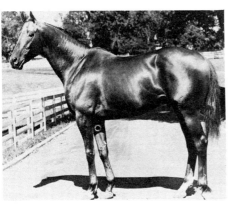

Thoroughbred Stallion

Quarter Horse Stallion

andardbred Stallion

American Saddle Horse

hetland Pony

elgian Stallion

Appaloosa Stallion

American Saddle Horse. This is one of the most popular breeds today because it gives an easy, comfortable ride and looks great while doing it. Most American saddle horses are used for recreational riding. They may be brown, chestnut, bay, gray, black, or golden in color. They weigh 1,000 to 1,200 pounds and stand from 15 to 16 hands high. (A horse's height is measured at the highest point of the withers; a hand is 4 inches.)

The American saddle horse was developed during the colonial days in Virginia, West Virginia, Kentucky, and Tennessee. The original stock included Thoroughbreds, Canadian pacers, Morgans, and Standardbreds. It was recognized as a

distinctive breed around 1900.

Appaloosa. The Appaloosa is a saddle horse noted for the colorful spots on its rear quarters. The original stock probably came to this continent with Spanish explorers. In the 19th century, most Appaloosas were owned by the Nez Percé Indian tribe of the Northwest, but the breed was widely scattered after the Indian wars. As Indian mounts, Appaloosas were used in war and buffalo hunting. Today they are mostly stock and pleasure horses.

Quarter Horse. The quarter horse gets its name from the fact that it developed out of horses which were raced over quarter-mile courses in the early days of our country. It is still raced on quarter-mile tracks, especially in the Southwest. But it is perhaps more important as a cow pony. The quarter horse is a well-muscled, agile animal that stands around 15 hands high. It weighs between 1,000 and 1,200 pounds. The most common colors are chestnut, sorrel, bay, and dun. The breed began developing in the southern states more than 300 years ago, but it is not certain what the foundation stocks were. Probably the beginning sire was a Thoroughbred stallion named Janus who lived from 1756 to 1780.

Shetland Pony. The smallest of all horses. (A pony must stand less than 14.2 hands and weigh 500 to 900 pounds.) Most Shetlands are less than 10.2 hands high and cannot be taller than 11.2. They come in almost all horse colors and are noted for their gentle disposition. Today the Shetland is used as a child's mount, show pony, and racer. The breed originated about 14 centuries ago in the Shetland Isles near Scotland.

Standardbred. In horse-and-buggy days, the Standardbred was the favorite road horse. He was a trotter and had great stamina along with good speed. Today the Standardbred is primarily a harness race horse, either at the pace or trot. The breed was developed in this country beginning in the 18th century from Thoroughbred stallions crossed with native mares. Standardbreds are a little smaller but more rugged than Thoroughbreds. They are from 15 to 16 hands in height and weigh 900 to 1,300 pounds. In color, they may be black, brown, bay, chestnut, gray, roan, or dun.

Thoroughbred. When we talk about racehorses, we usually mean Thoroughbreds. (Unless, that is, we're referring to trotting or pacing.) The Thoroughbred was developed in England for racing and did not arrive in our country until the 18th century. Thoroughbreds usually are bay, brown, black, or chestnut and often have white markings. They may be 15 to 17 hands in height. While racing, most weigh 900 to 1,025 pounds, although stallions may grow much heavier in stud. They tend to be nervous and excitable. Although nearly all Thoroughbreds are bred for racing, some are also used as saddle horses and polo mounts.

Draft Horse. This is not a breed but a type of horse which includes several breeds. The draft horse was the tractor and truck of the 19th century and before. Today few draft horses are work animals, but some are kept for show. Draft horses stand 16 to 17 hands in height and weigh from 1,600 to more than 2,000 pounds. The most popular breeds today are the Belgian, Percheron, Shire, and Clydesdale.

Dairy Cattle

Most of the dairy cattle in the United States belong to five chief breeds—Ayrshire, Brown Swiss, Guernsey, Holstein, and Jersey. Some breeds give more milk while others have a higher percent butterfat test. So you should pick the breed that best fits your conditions and markets.

Some areas have developed a market demand for high butterfat milk and milk products, so the producer may want a herd that gives much butterfat. Or there may be a strong market for calves producing meat, so the producer should consider the growth rate of a breed's calves. He should also ask himself what breeds are grown by other dairymen in his area. If he's thinking about Ayrshires and everybody else has Holsteins, how will he get rid of surplus animals?

Another important factor is the producer's own preference. Whatever breed he chooses, though, he should always try to get good *individual* animals. And naturally he will then try to improve his herd by breeding and good care.

The five chief breeds of dairy cattle have different average levels of milk and butterfat production. For total pounds of milk produced, they rank as follows: Holstein, Brown Swiss, Ayrshire, Guernsey, and Jersey. For butterfat test, the ranking is exactly opposite, with Jerseys highest and Holsteins lowest.

Milking Shorthorn Cow

Ayrshire Bull

Brown Swiss Cow

Guernsey Cow

Holstein Cow

Jersey Cow

Ayrshire. This breed is most numerous in the Northeast. Ayrshires are well built and stocky with symmetrical udders which are well-attached to the body. Horns are wide and curve up and out. (There are polled, or unhorned, animals, too.) At birth, calves weigh 60 to 80 pounds. Ayrshires are usually light to deep cherry red, mahogany, or brown, or a combination of colors; some are white. The breed originated in Scotland.

Brown Swiss. As the name indicates, the breed was developed in Switzerland. In the U.S. they are found chiefly in North Central and Eastern states. Brown Swiss are well muscled and rugged and tend to be calm and unexcitable. Calves weigh 65 to 90 pounds at birth. Heifers are slow to mature. In color they are solid brown, varying from very light to dark.

Guernsey. This breed is found throughout the U.S., but is most numerous in the Central States. Guernseys are medium-sized cattle, with a mature cow in milk weighing about 1,100 pounds. Calves weigh 55 to 85 pounds at birth. Heifers mature early. Their milk is especially yellow in color. They are gentle and easily handled. Guernseys are fawn-colored with white markings; their horns are medium-length and incline forward. Skin color is golden yellow or pinkish. The breed originated on the Isle of Guernsey off the north coast of France.

Holstein. This is the most popular breed in the U.S. and appears in all states. It is also the largest breed, with mature cows weighing about 1,500 pounds. Holsteins are black-and-white. Calves weigh 70 to 105 pounds at birth. Because of its high milk production, the breed is especially popular in market milk areas. Holsteins are descended from cattle developed in the northern part of the Netherlands, especially the province of Friesland, and northern Germany.

Jersey. This is the smallest of the five common breeds, with mature cows in milk weighing about 1,000 pounds. Jerseys are found in every state. Calves weigh 40 to 75 pounds at birth. Heifers mature rapidly. The breed has well-shaped udders. In color, Jerseys vary greatly, but most are some shade of fawn, often with white markings. The breed was developed on the Island of Jersey between England and France.

Dual-Purpose Breeds. Some breeds of cattle are kept for both milk production and good beef. Most prominent of these breeds are the Milking Shorthorn and the Red Poll. They are favorites of farmers who don't want to specialize in either dairying or beef production.

Beef Cattle

Dairy cattle and beef cattle are brothers and sisters under the skin. But while dairy cattle are bred to be big producers of milk, beef cattle are bred for their meat. Beef cattle should have wide and deep bodies with firm, thick flesh. Dairy cattle are leaner and more angular, but must have well-developed udders.

As is true for dairy cattle, there is no one "best" breed of beef cattle. The cattleman usually makes his choice of breed based on personal preference. Often, though, it is best to raise the breed that is most numerous in your area so that animals can be exchanged and there can be cooperation among breeders.

More important than the choice of breed is the choice of individuals within the breed.

Aberdeen-Angus, or *Angus.* This breed is easily recognized because it is all black. It is polled (unhorned). Angus tend to be slightly lighter than Herefords and Shorthorns but the body is compact, broad, and well muscled. Angus mature early and have high-quality meat. The breed is very popular in the Central, Southern, and Western States. Angus cattle were developed in northern Scotland and were first brought to the United States in 1873.

Hereford. A favorite all over the U.S., the Hereford is by far the most popular breed. It is especially favored in the West and Southwest because it is an excellent range animal due to its foraging ability. Herefords are strong, vigorous animals with deep, wide, well-fleshed bodies. They always have white faces, and the body color is a medium to rich red, with white on underparts. The breed originated in England and arrived in the U.S. in 1817.

Polled Hereford. The basic difference between Herefords and this breed is that Polled Herefords are hornless. The breed was developed in the U.S. in the early years of this century from Herefords which were born polled.

Shorthorn. The largest of the common beef breeds, the Shorthorn is widespread in the U.S. but particularly in the Corn Belt. Most Shorthorn cows are good milkers, and so their calves tend to grow rapidly. In color, they may be all red, all white, or any combination of red and white; roans are most numerous. Shorthorns are an old breed, dating back to the 16th century. They first came to this country in 1783.

Polled Shorthorn. Like the Polled Hereford, the Polled Shorthorn was developed in the U.S. It differs from the Shorthorn only in its lack of horns. It may, however, be spotted.

Other Breeds. The five breeds listed above are the most numerous in this country. Others that are well-represented are Brahman, Santa Gertrudis, Charolais, Galloway, Devon, Charbray, and Brangus. In addition, there are the dual-purpose breeds—the Milking Shorthorn and Red Poll.

Exotic Breeds of Cattle: Some of these are Simmental, Limousin, Chianna, Maine-Anjou, Charlois, and Charbrays. They are being extensively imported into the United States. The interest in these breeds is due to their ability to mature at an early age, to develop larger loin eyes, produce less fat, make more economical gains in weight, and produce a higher percentage of red meat. These cattle are being bred as pure breeds and also crossed with other breeds of cattle found in the United States.

Polled Shorthorn Cow

Angus Bull

Shorthorn Cow

Polled Hereford Bull

Hereford Cow

Sheep

There are about 200 breeds of sheep, but only a dozen are of commercial importance in the United States. The important breeds may be grouped into two types: the fine-wool type, raised mainly for its wool, and the mutton type, for meat. The chief fine-wool types are the American merino, Delaine merino, and Rambouillet. Mutton types include sheep also classified as "medium wool" and "long wool." (It should be understood that all types of sheep provide both wool and mutton, but each breed is noted for quality of one or the other.) Among the most common mutton types are Suffolk, Hampshire, Corriedale, Dorset, Southdown, Shropshire, Columbia, Cheviot, and Oxford.

Sheep farmers make their choice of breed based on a number of factors. An important one is the market. The producer must ask himself: Is the market better for wool or for mutton? Also important are the climate, the size of the farm, available feed, and manpower. Various breeds differ in their herding instinct, for example. Fine-wool breeds tend to herd better, which means that they are more adapted to the open range than most mutton types.

Columbia Ram

Delaine Marino Ram

Shropshire Ewe

Southdown Ram

Suffolk Ram

Rambouillet Ram

Hampshire Ewe

Cheviot Ram

Dorset Ram

Corriedale Ram

Oxford Ram

Lincoln Ram

Cheviot. This is a small, hardy sheep with excellent mutton. Mature rams weigh 160 to 200 pounds and ewes 120 to 160. Fleece weight is usually light, about five to seven pounds. The face and legs have no wool. Cheviots originated in the border country between Scotland and England and arrived in the U.S. in 1838.

Columbia. This is a breed developed in America by crossing long-wool and fine-wool breeds. Mature rams weigh 225 to 275 pounds and ewes 125 to 190. Both sexes are polled. The face and legs are covered with white hair. Columbia ewes produce a wool clip of 11 to 13 pounds. The breed herds well and so is well-adapted to open ranges.

Corriedale. Another crossbred, the Corriedale, was developed in New Zealand in the 19th century. It pro-

vides both good mutton and dense fleece of good quality. Mature rams weigh 185 to 225 pounds, and ewes range from 125 to 185. Both sexes are polled. Corriedales shear 10 to 12 pounds of wool per year.

Dorset. This breed, which originated in England, is noted for producing "hothouse," or winter, lambs and is most popular east of the Mississippi River. Twins and triplets are common. Dorsets are of medium size, with rams weighing 175 to 200 pounds and ewes from 125 to 175. Both sexes are horned. They are light-wool producers.

Hampshire. This popular breed produces excellent mutton. Its fleece is of medium quality and usually from 6 to 12 pounds. The Hampshire is large, with rams weighing from 225 to 300 pounds and ewes 150 to 200. The face and legs of the Hampshire are deep brown or black. Lambs grow very rapidly. Both sexes are hornless.

Merino. There are three types of this breed— "A" and "B" types of American merino and the "C," or Delaine merino. They differ chiefly in the degree of skin folds or wrinkles. The smoothest skin is on the Delaine merino, which is now the most popular type. Delaine merinos produce the best quality wool in this country. Merinos are strong and hardy and herd very well. Mature rams of the Delaine type weigh from 150 to 200 pounds and ewes from 110 to 150. Most rams are horned. The merino originated in Spain and was first imported into the U.S. in the 18th century.

Oxford. This is the largest of the medium-wool sheep, with rams weighing 250 to 350 pounds and ewes 175 to 250. Both sexes are polled. They shear heavier than other medium-wool breeds, with 10 to 12 pounds about average. The breed was developed in south central England and arrived in this country in 1846.

Rambouillet. This is a large breed of good wool producers which also offers acceptable mutton. Rambouillets herd well and are very popular in range country. Rams weigh 225 to 275 pounds and ewes from 140 to 200. Most rams have large, spiral horns, but some are polled. It is believed that about half

of all sheep in the U.S. carry some Rambouillet breeding. The breed is descended entirely from the Spanish Merino and came to the U.S. in the 19th century.

Shropshire. This breed is often called a "middle-of-the-road" breed because it has good mutton and is one of the heaviest wool producers among medium-wool sheep. In size, it ranks between the Southdown and Hampshire. Shearing brings about 8 to 12 pounds of wool annually. Its lambs grow rapidly, although not as fast as Southdowns. Shropshires were developed in England and first appeared in this country about 1855.

Southdown. An excellent breed for mutton, the Southdown also produces fine-quality wool—but in small amounts. It has a compact body with deep and firm flesh. Rams weigh 175 to 225 pounds and ewes 125 to 160. Both sexes are polled. The lambs mature early. This breed is favored by many 4-H club and FFA members. The Southdown is a native of southeastern England and had arrived in the U.S. by the 17th century.

Suffolk. Another mutton breed, the Suffolk was developed in England by crossing Southdown rams with ewes from an English breed called Norfolk. The Suffolk has a very black face, ears, and legs. It is about the size of the Hampshire. Both sexes are hornless. Lambs mature rapidly.

Hogs

Most swine producers today try to breed hogs that are neither immense nor small. Rather, they want the "meat" type with a good yield of the lean cuts—ham, loin, picnic shoulder, and Boston butt cuts. The best specimens are well muscled and have a low ratio of fat. Some breeds, however, are noted for their bacon; these tend to have even less fat than the meat type.

As is true for other livestock, there is no "best" breed of hog. A hog producer must consider the growth rate of the breed, how many pigs are in an average litter, the desirability of the meat, and of course, his own preference.

About 20 breeds are common in the United States today.

American Landrace. This breed was developed as a bacon-type hog in Denmark and was first brought here in 1934. The Landrace is white; some animals have spots or freckles. Mature boars weigh 700 to 900 pounds and sows 550 to 750. The Landrace has a long body and rather short legs.

Berkshire. An English breed, the Berkshire is one of the oldest improved breeds. It first came to the U.S. in 1823. A mature Berkshire is of medium size, with boars weighing 700 to 900 pounds and sows 600 to 750. The breed is long-bodied and produces fine quality meat. Berk-

Yorkshire Sow

Tamworth Barrow

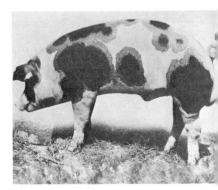

Spotted Poland China

American Landrace Boar

Berkshire Gilt

Chester White Gilt

Duroc Gilt

Hampshire Barrow

Poland China Gilt

shires are black with white on the face, tail, and all four feet.

Chester White. Today's Chester White weighs 600 to 700 pounds at maturity—a far cry from his ancestors, who often dressed out at more than 1,000 pounds. The sows have large litters, and the pigs mature early, developing excellent meat. The breed was developed in Chester and Delaware counties in Pennsylvania early in the 19th century. It is popular in Northern States.

Duroc. The leading breed in the U.S., the Duroc originated in New Jersey and New York in the mid-1800's. Durocs are all red, although the shade varies from light to dark. It is a hardy breed with good feeding capacity and large size. Boars weigh from 750 to 1,100 pounds and sows 600 to 850. Pigs reach market weight of about 200 pounds beginning at about 5 months.

Hampshire. This breed is recognized by its black body with a white belt running over the shoulders and front legs. The Hampshire is relatively small, with boars weighing 600 to 850 pounds and sows 500 to 700. Hampshires are trim and smooth-bodied with little excess fat. The breed was developed from English breeds in Boone County, Kentucky, during the 19th century.

Poland China. The name of this breed is misleading since it is likely that its ancestors were from nei-

ther Poland nor China. It was developed in the late 19th century in Butler and Warren counties, Ohio. Most Poland Chinas are black, many with white spots on the feet, snout, and tail. Mature boars weigh 850 to 1,000 pounds and sows 650 to 900.

Spotted. This breed is a cousin of the Poland China and resembles it in most respects. The spotted is slightly smaller on the average than the Poland China. The other major difference is coloring. The ideal spotted is 50 percent white and 50 percent black.

Tamworth. This is a bacon-type breed and one of the oldest of the

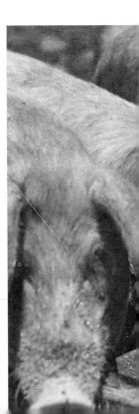

purebreds. Tamworths originated in Ireland and were further developed in England. They came to the U.S. in 1882. The color is light to dark red. They have a high proportion of lean meat, especially bacon, and produce large litters of pigs. Boars weigh from 700 to 1,000 pounds and sows from 550 to 750.

Yorkshire. Native to England, the Yorkshire is noted as an excellent bacon breed. The body is long, deep, and smooth, with large loins. The color is white, occasionally with black freckles. Boars weigh from 700 to 1,000 pounds and sows from 500 to 800. The meat is of very good quality.

Hybrid Swine: In addition to the pure breeds of swine, there have been developed hybrid breeds which are popular among farmers to raise for consumer use. The Landrace breed has been used extensively in crossing with such breeds as the Berkshire, Poland China, Chester White, and Hampshire. The resulting hybrids are known as Maryland No. 1, Beltsville No. 1, LaCombe Minnesota No. 1, and Montana No. 1, respectively. The advantages of such hybrid breeds are greater feed efficiency, meatier with less fat, larger loin eyes, and feeder pigs which are marketed at an earlier age.

Livestock Diseases and Treatment

Whatever kind of animals he raises, the livestock producer must constantly be on guard against disease. His livelihood depends on sound, healthy stock. And so the producer must know something about the diseases, parasites, and ailments that afflict his animals.

Each year, losses from diseases and parasites run into the millions of dollars. Much of this loss probably could be averted by timely measures of prevention and control.

There is an old saying that "an ounce of prevention is worth a pound of cure." It certainly applies to the livestock industry. In a later chapter we will discuss the importance of good management in preventing disease.

In this chapter, we will look at a few of the common diseases of livestock. Talk with your merit badge counselor or county agent about the most serious diseases in your area. Also, refer to the books about particular species in the last chapter of this pamphlet.

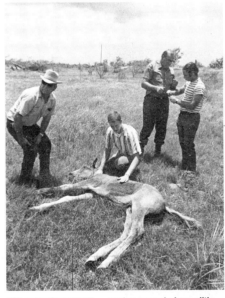

"Sleeping Sickness" — equine encephalomyelitis

Diseases of Horses

Often the first sign of disease in a horse is high temperature, a rapid pulse rate, or rapid breathing. The normal ranges are:

Temperature—99-100.8° F., with 100.5 average.

Pulse—32 to 44 beats per minute.

Breathing—8 to 16 times per minute.

A horse's temperature is taken with an animal thermometer inserted in the rectum. *You should get instruction from an expert before trying to take a horse's temperature.*

The pulse rate is taken by feeling an artery at the margin of the jaw, the inside of the elbow, or under the tail. Count the breathing rate by placing your hand on the horse's flank. Remember that temperature, pulse, and breathing rate may be affected by exercise, excitement, and hot weather.

Distemper (Strangles). This disease is widespread, particularly among young horses. It should be treated promptly by a veterinarian. The first symptoms are depression and loss of appetite, followed by high temperature and a discharge of pus from the nose. Three or four days after onset the glands under the jaw begin getting

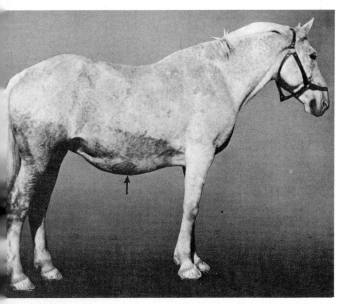

Acute "Swamp Fever" — Infectious Anemia

bigger. Eventually they break open and discharge pus. The horse may cough frequently. If distemper spreads to other glands, it is called lymph strangles.

Distemper is caused by bacteria present in the air or the animal's feed. It can be prevented by avoiding contact with infected animals and stables and equipment they have used. An infected horse must be quarantined and given clean, fresh water, good feed and good shelter. Antibiotics and sulfa drugs should be given by a veterinarian.

Encephalomyelitis (Sleeping sickness, brain fever). This is an infectious brain disease occurring from early summer to the first hard frost. The first symptom is aimlessness. The horse wanders around, crashing into objects. Later it may appear sleepy and stand with its head down. It may grind its teeth or fall as local paralysis develops. In severe cases, the horse may die within four days. Some animals recover fully; others only partially.

Encephalomyelitis is caused by four different viruses, two of which are important in the United States. The virus is transmitted by inhalation and by the bites of various species of mosquitos and two other insects.

As soon as the disease appears, all horses in the area should be vaccinated. This should be done by a veterinarian. The disease is treated by good nursing, including fresh water and feed. Medicines may also

be used in treatment.

Equine Abortion. About one-third of all pregnant mares abort or produce weak, infected foals. So this is a serious problem for the horse breeder. Abortions are caused by four kinds of bacteria and viruses, and also by such things as accidents, injuries, and defective development of the fetus.

Prevention of abortion involves vaccination and inoculation against diseases, mating only healthy stallion and mares, and keeping broodmares well fed and in good flesh.

Symptoms of possible abortion may be any illness in a pregnant mare which cannot be accounted for. A veterinarian should be called at once. With proper treatment, many abortions can be prevented.

Swamp Fever. This is a serious blood disease with the scientific name of equine infectious anemia. It has various symptoms. Often there is high temperature, depression, stiffness, weakness in the hindquarters, swelling of the lower body and legs, unthriftiness, and loss of condition and weight. Swamp fever can be diagnosed but there is no known treatment.

The disease is caused by a virus which is spread chiefly by biting insects, especially flies. It may be carried by infected horses for a long time.

When a definite diagnosis has been made, the horse should be killed and the carcass destroyed.

Diseases of Cattle

The same diseases strike both dairy and beef cattle, so they will be considered together. (A few diseases that infect the udder are, of course, more serious in dairy cattle.)

As with horses, the first signs of illness in cattle often are high temperature, rapid pulse, and rapid breathing. For cattle, normal rates are:

Temperature—100.4-102.8° F., with 101.5 average.

Pulse—60-70 beats per minute.

Breathing—10-30 times per minute.

An animal thermometer should be used to take the temperature of cattle. The thermometer is inserted in the rectum. *You should get instruction from an expert before trying to take an animal's temperature.* Take the pulse of cattle on the outside of the jaw just above its lower border, on the soft area just above the inner dewclaw, or just above the hock joint. Check the breathing rate by placing a hand on the flank. Remember that temperature, pulse, and breathing rate may be affected by exercise, excitement, and hot weather.

Anthrax. This is an acute, infectious disease that can strike all warm-blooded animals and man. It is most often seen in mature cattle. Because most cattle in affected regions are vaccinated, it does not often occur. But when it does, it may hit hundreds of animals.

Infected animals tend to begin staggering, have trouble breathing, tremble, and collapse. Temperature soars, milk production drops, and pregnant cows often abort.

Anthrax is caused by a bacillus which may remain in the soil for long periods. When the disease is suspected, a veterinarian should be called at once. Infected animals must be quarantined and all others vaccinated.

Blackleg. A widespread disease, particularly in the western range states. Blackleg is highly fatal and is seen most often in 3-month to 2-year-old cattle.

The disease is caused by a strain of bacteria that infect an open wound or are ingested with feed. The first symptom is lameness, and this is accompanied by swellings over the neck, shoulder, flanks, thigh, and breast. Temperature is usually high and the animal loses its appetite. Death generally occurs within 3 days, although a few animals recover. With proper care by a veterinarian, older animals may be treated successfully.

The best preventive step is vaccination of all animals.

Bloat. A widespread ailment that causes annual losses of nearly $50 million in dairy cattle alone. It occurs when gas builds up in the first two compartments (rumen and reticulum) of the stomach of cattle and other ruminant animals. The symptom is a big paunch on the animal's left side in front of the

27

Animal dead of Blackleg

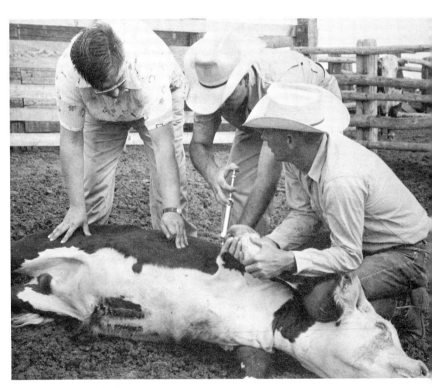

Vaccination for Brucellosis

hip bone. The cause is unknown, although dairymen know that some families of animals get it more often than others, and that animals feeding in legume pastures are especially susceptible.

Severe cases should be treated by a veterinarian. Mild cases may be treated by keeping the animal on its feet and moving and by drenching through a stomach tube with vegetable oil.

Brucellosis (Bang's Disease). This disease affects cattle, swine, goats, and man through three different organisms. It hits the dairy industry particularly hard because it makes abortion frequent, causes other ailments, and cuts milk production. In addition, there is always danger of passing the disease to man.

Brucellosis is difficult to diagnose because symptoms are indefinite. The most common symptom is abortion.

Preventive measures include sound herd management and vaccination of calves, checking of milk samples regularly, and blood tests if the disease is suspected. There is no known medicine that is effective against brucellosis. Infected animals must be slaughtered or quarantined.

Shipping fever (Hemorrhagic Septicemia or Stockyard Fever). This is an acute respiratory disease among cattle and is most common in young stock and those that have been shipped. Rising body temperature, discharge from nose and eyes, hacking cough, and difficult breathing are common symptoms. Cause is attributed to an interaction of a virus and stressful environmental agents such as change in weather and feed, overcrowding, and lack of rest. To prevent and minimize this disease, all cattle should be vaccinated with a shipping-fever vaccine prior to shipping.

Anthraxed heifer carcass ready for cremation

Diseases of Sheep

Like horses and cattle, sheep often show early symptoms of illness by high temperature, rapid pulse, and rapid breathing. Here are the norms for sheep:

Temperature—100.9-103.8° F., with 102.3 average.

Pulse—70-80 beats per minute.

Breathing—12-20 times per minute.

Temperatures should be taken with an animal thermometer inserted in the rectum. *You should get instruction from an expert before trying to take an animal's temperature.*

Temperature and pulse and breathing rates are affected by exercise, excitement, age of the animal, and outside temperature.

Sheep are prey to diseases that affect other animals, including anthrax, blackleg, and brucellosis. Other common diseases follow.

Taking blood samples for test purposes

Arthritis. There are two types of this disease of lambs. One is called swine erysipelas. Most lambs recover from it within a month without treatment. The other is called suppurative arthritis and is more serious. Recovery chances are poor and animals that live usually are crippled.

Symptoms of both types are lameness, high temperature, listlessness, and poor appetite. In the more serious type, there is a marked swelling of affected joints with pus in the joint cavities. No satisfactory treatment is known, although sometimes antibiotics or sulfa drugs prescribed by a veterinarian are of value.

Chances of the disease's occurring are lessened by careful attention to cleanliness in ranges, pastures, and lambing quarters.

Enterotoxemia. Sometimes called overeating disease, this illness can occur in sheep of all ages being fed on lush feed of grain, milk, or grass. Affected sheep lose their appetite and become sluggish. They have diarrhea and often stagger about blindly. Infected sheep may die within a few hours after the first signs are noticed.

Enterotoxemia is caused by a toxin produced by a strain of bacteria found in the soil and in the digestive tract of most warm-blooded animals.

Preventive treatment consists of administering a toxoid.

Pneumonia. One of the most common sheep diseases, pneumonia shows itself by high fever, difficult breathing, and refusal to eat. Occasionally older sheep die of this disease without showing any symptoms.

It may be caused by bacteria, viruses, or lungworm parasites. But it usually develops after chilling or poor feeding. Sulfonamides and antibiotics are used in treatment, but they are not effective against the lungworm variety.

Many instances of pneumonia can be prevented by good management, particularly adequate shelter.

Sore Mouth (Contagious Ecthyma).
Sore mouth is rarely fatal, but it causes great economic losses because growth of lambs is retarded. Infected lambs first show symptoms of depression and refusal to eat. Small blisters or cysts will be seen on lips, gums, and tongue, and when they break they bleed easily and form sores. They may heal in 4 to 18 days, but meanwhile the animal stays off its feed.

Sore mouth is caused by a virus. Treatment includes vaccination and sometimes isolation of the infected sheep.

Spraying for lice

Diseases of Hogs

Swine are susceptible to a number of diseases affecting other livestock (and some that affect man), including anthrax, brucellosis, foot-and-mouth disease, pneumonia, and tuberculosis. The diseases listed below are among the most common in hogs.

Most infectious diseases of hogs (and other animals) result in high temperatures and often rapid pulse or rapid breathing. The rates below are normal for swine:

Temperature—102-103.6° F., with 102.6 average.

Pulse—60-80 beats per minute

Breathing—8-18 breaths per minute.

Temperatures should be taken with an animal thermometer inserted in the rectum. *You should get instruction from an expert before trying to take an animal's temperature.*

Remember that body temperature, pulse rate, and breathing rate are affected by exercise, excitement, age and size of the animal, and outside temperature.

Atrophic Rhinitis. This is a widespread disease in the United States and appears to affect swine only. The first symptom is persistent sneezing in young pigs. When an infected pig is 4 to 8 weeks old, its snout begins to wrinkle, and it may thicken. By the time the pig is 4 months old, the snout and face may be twisted to one side. The animals make slow weight gains and some-

times die of pneumonia brought on by this disease.

Atrophic rhinitis seems to be caused by bacteria and may also be due to calcium deficiency or imbalance in calcium and phosphorus intake.

Several control plans are suggested, including selecting clean breeding stock, buying pigs above 60 to 80 pounds in weight, and maintaining clean farrowing quarters.

Hog Cholera. This is among the most serious swine diseases. It is highly contagious. The usual symptoms are high temperature, weakness, and loss of appetite. Often infected animals leave the herd and show a wobbly gait. They drink much water and cough frequently. Constipation alternates with diarrhea, and there may be a discharge from the eyes.

There is no effective treatment, and infected and exposed hogs must be destroyed.

Mycoplasma Pneumonia. This disease causes swine producers great losses because, although an infected pig's appetite remains good, he gains weight slowly. The first symptom is usually coughing, particularly in the early morning and following exercise. Some pigs develop pneumonia while suffering from this disease.

It is caused by a bacillus which spreads from animal to animal in a herd. It is treated with various drugs by veterinarians.

Pig Scours. Between 7 million and

10 million suckling pigs die of this disease in the United States each year. It is an acute disease characterized by creamy-yellow or grayish-green, watery feces. It spreads from pig to pig within a litter. Sows are not affected.

Several organisms are believed to cause pig scours. The disease usually occurs in conditions of poor sanitation, drafts or dust, dampness, chilling, and poor diet. Drugs are usually effective in controlling pig scours.

Swine dysentery. This is an acute infectious disease, prevalent in all parts of the United States. It is referred to by many names, such as bloody diarrhea, bloody sours, bloody dysentery, black sours, or hemorrhagic enteritis. Outbreaks of the disease are usually associated with animals that pass through central markets or public auctions. However, it is not uncommon to find the disease on breeding farms that are not following strict sanitary management practices. A characteristic symptom of swine dysentery is a profuse bloody diarrhea, sometimes black rather than red. Animals stop eating and their body temperature rises. Death can occur among some pigs within a few days of the illness, while others linger several weeks and then die. The disease is highly contagious and sick animals should be isolated.

Advanced Hog Cholera

Digestive Systems of Livestock

Feed is the most important factor in growth, health, and productivity of all kinds of livestock. It is also a big expense on any livestock farm or ranch. For most types of livestock, feed is the *biggest* expense.

The livestock producer must feed his animals well, but he must keep his costs down if he is to make a profit. Both good nutrition and economy can be achieved if the stockman understands how his animals digest their food and how it is converted into profitable meat, milk, eggs, or wool.

The digestive systems of farm animals are of two kinds: ruminant and nonruminant.

Ruminants are the cud-chewing, cloven-hoofed animals, including cattle, sheep, and goats. (Wild ruminants are deer, bison, antelope, camel, giraffe, llama, and a few others.) All other livestock, including fowl, are classified as nonruminants.

The chief difference between ruminant and nonruminant animals is that the ruminant's stomach has four compartments, while the nonruminant's has only one. The result is that their feed needs are quite different, even though both types of animals need proteins, carbohydrates and fats, minerals, vitamins, and water.

Let's start with the nonruminants.

Digestion in Nonruminants

The digestive process of simple-stomached animals is similar to that of man. In fact, that of a pig bears a very strong resemblance, and so the nutritional needs of man and pig are much alike. (See diagrams.)

Now we will follow the digestive process of a typical nonruminant—the horse. The process starts in the mouth, where the food is chewed by the horse's 24 molars and 12 incisor teeth and moistened with saliva. The saliva makes the food's passage down the esophagus easier and it also contains an enzyme that begins breaking the feed down into its elements.

The esophagus is a 50- to 60-inch-long tube leading to the stomach. Gastric juices in the stomach, which holds 8 to 16 quarts, begin breaking down fats and proteins so that they can be absorbed into the bloodstream. In the small intestine, which is about 7 feet long, enzymes continue to break down the protein, fats, and sugars. The large intestine has four parts: the cecum, great colon, small colon, and rectum. Digestion and absorption of

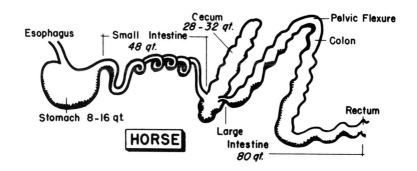

Esophagus — Small Intestine
48 qt.

Cecum
28 - 32 qt.

Pelvic Flexure

Colon

Stomach 8-16 qt.

Rectum

HORSE

Large
Intestine
80 qt.

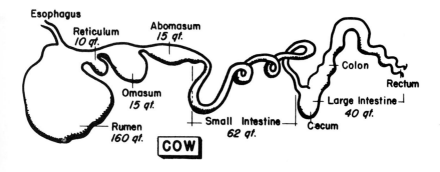

Esophagus

Reticulum
10 qt.

Abomasum
15 qt.

Colon

Rectum

Omasum
15 qt.

Small Intestine
62 qt.

Large Intestine
40 qt.

Cecum

Rumen
160 qt.

COW

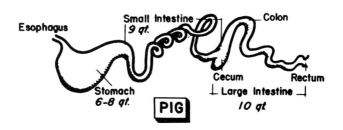

Esophagus

Small Intestine
9 qt.

Colon

Stomach
6-8 qt.

Cecum

Rectum

PIG

Large Intestine
10 qt.

nutrients continue as the food passes through the cecum and great colon. In the small colon, waste becomes solid in balls of dung, which are expelled through the rectum.

For its size, the horse has a small stomach. This means that it must eat small amounts over a long period instead of large amounts in a short time. If a horse is not fed, its stomach will be empty within 24 hours. (A ruminant's stomach takes 72 hours to empty.)

Digestion in Ruminants

The drawing shows the digestive "plumbing" of a ruminant—the cow—as it would look stretched out. Actually, it winds around inside the body in more complicated fashion.

Digestion begins in the mouth, where the cow's 32 teeth (eight of which are incisors in the lower jaw) chew the food. A heavy flow of saliva mixes with the food to aid in swallowing. The food then travels down the esophagus to the rumen, or paunch. A little of it may bypass the rumen and go directly to the reticulum.

The rumen, which in a mature cow holds 160 quarts, has several purposes. One is to act as a storage place for food. When the cow finishes feeding, she will regurgitate the larger particles back into her mouth and chew them more completely. The rumen also breaks down food particles further and continues the digestive process.

The reticulum looks somewhat like a honeycomb. Its main job is to screen out nonfood matter. Next stop is the omasum, which is lined with folds of tissue. Its function seems to be to cut down water content of the food and continue grinding it.

The food next passes into the fourth compartment—the abomasum. This is the "true stomach," and its action and purpose are much like that in a nonruminant. The small and large intestines of ruminant animals have the same functions as in nonruminants.

Mainly because of their digestive systems, ruminant animals can go for longer periods without food than nonruminants, provided that they have adequate rations when they *are* fed. Ruminants are also able to eat more roughage, such as grass and legumes, which require more digestive action than grains and other feeds.

CAPACITIES OF DIGESTIVE TRACTS (in quarts)

	Horse	Cow	Pig
Stomach	8-16	(200)	6-8
Rumen		160	
Reticulum		10	
Omasum		15	
Abomasum		15	
Small intestine	48	62	9
Cecum	28-32		
Large intestine	80	40	10

Good Management Practices

Like humans, animals have certain physical needs that must be met if they are to develop normally, stay healthy, and be productive.

For livestock, the needs include feeding and watering, sanitary housing, exercise, and, for some kinds, regular grooming. Veterinarians believe that at least three-fourths of the losses from death (and lowered production) in farm animals could be prevented if these needs were met adequately.

Proper management practices are different for different stock. Cattle and sheep have the same basic needs, but the way they are met is not the same. In this section we will cover these needs in general terms. For more detailed information, talk with your merit badge counselor, county extension agent, or a livestock producer. You will also find help in the list of resources in the chapter called "Resources for Your Specialty" in this booklet.

Feeding and Watering

Fresh, clean water is a must at all times for every kind of animal. The watering equipment should be kept sparkling clean by daily scrubbings and exposure to sunlight.

A balanced diet is also essential to health. Different kinds of animals vary in their nutritional needs, but all require some of the following:

- **Carbohydrates.** Sugars, starches, cellulose, fats, and oils. They provide energy.
- **Proteins.** Complex compounds of carbon, hydrogen, oxygen, nitrogen, sulfur, phosphorus, and iron. Proteins make up the body tissues and ensure good health.
- **Vitamins.** Complex substances found in most foods and diet supplements. They are vital to health.
- **Minerals.** Iron, copper, phosphorus, potassium, calcium, and iodine. They are also vital to health and perform important functions.
- **Water.** Hydrogen and oxygen. Water is the most important of all and makes up most of the animal's weight.

Without a balanced diet of all these nutrients, animals are prey to many diseases. Horses with poor diets may give birth to weak or deformed foals and suffer from founder (laminitis) and many forms of lameness. Cattle may get milk fever, ketosis, indigestion, white muscle disease, grass tetany, rickets, or night blindness. Swine develop anemia, ulcers, and scours and may have dead litters. Poultry may suffer from a drop in egg production or lay eggs that won't hatch.

Horses. The feed requirements of horses depend on age and size of the animal and also on the amount of work they do. Racing horses need greater amounts than pleasure horses or those that are idle.

The following figures will give you an idea of the differences:

Suggested daily feeding for 1,000-pound light horse exposed to light activity:

Ration #1
Alfalfa hay 10 lb.
Oats 4 lb.

Ration #2
Grass hay 14 lb.
Oats 5 lb.

Ration #3
Alfalfa hay 10 lb.
Oats 3 lb.
Barley 1 lb.

Daily ration for 1,200-pound brood mare and stallion in service:

Ration #1
Alfalfa hay 14-16 lb.
Oats 10 lb.
Mineral supplement
2 oz.

Ration #2
Alfalfa hay 10 lb.
Grass hay 4 lb.
Oats 5 lb.
Corn 3 lb.
Barley 2 lb.
Wheat bran 2 lb.

Ration #3
Grass hay 8 lb.
Alfalfa hay 5 lb.
Oats 12 lb.
Wheat germ oil 1 oz.
Mineral supplement 2 oz.

Dairy Cattle. Rations for dairy cattle depend on age and size, whether cows are in milk or are pregnant, and how much milk is being produced. The following are rules of thumb for daily rations:
• Growing heifers need one-quarter to one-third pound of grains and protein concentrates combined per 100 pounds live weight, plus legume roughage at will.

- Dry cows need 20 pounds of corn silage and other roughage at will; or 4 pounds of grain and concentrates and roughage at will; or run on pasture.
- Milking cows need 2 pounds of legume hay, or 1 pound of legume hay and 3 pounds of corn silage per 100 pounds of live weight, plus grains and concentrates depending on the amount of milk they produce.

Beef Cattle. As with dairy cattle, rations for beef cattle will vary depending on the animal's age and size. The following are rules of thumb:

- On full feed, cattle will eat about 60 percent grains and concentrates, 40 percent roughages. Pasture is an excellent source of feed, and beef cattle can gain from ¾ to 1¼ pounds per day. On full grain feed, they gain from 1½ to 2½ pounds.
- On full feed, a steer will eat about 1½ to 2 pounds of grain and concentrates per 100 pounds live weight. He will eat 1 pound of hay per 100 pounds of weight.

Sheep. Probably 95 percent of a sheep's feed is obtained from roughages. Sheep are somewhat less finicky eaters than other live-

stock, but they always thrive best on good pastures and properly balanced rations.

Generally, ewes require 4½ to 5 pounds of dry feed or its equivalent each day. It is made up of legume hay, grass hay and silage, or merely a good pasture. Often ½ to 1½ pounds of grain is added to the diet of ewes during pregnancy, after birth, and just before breeding.

Hogs. Both underfeeding and overfeeding of hogs should be avoided. Underfed hogs will grow too slowly, and if they are overfed, some of the feed is wasted and the danger of illness in increased.

Some swine producers use these rules of thumb:

- Give 1 pound of feed for each 30 pounds of body weight from 120 pounds to market weight.
- Feed only the amount eaten in 20 to 30 minutes.
- Feed 70 to 90 percent of full feed.

Finishing hogs, while on full feed, will eat 4 to 6 pounds of feed, mostly concentrates, each day per 100 pounds live weight.

Housing

Every kind of livestock needs some sort of protection against severe weather and predators, for times of illness, and for its young.

The kind of shelter that is needed depends on the type of livestock, its size and feeding habits, and the climate. In every case where barns or other living quarters must be provided for animals, they should be clean and dry, free of drafts, and with no sharp edges or nails that might injure animals.

Good drainage is important, and all waste material should be removed regularly and spread on unused animal pastures where it will be dried by the sun. This treatment kills disease-carrying organisms, and the wastes provide valuable nutrients for the soil.

Exercise

Daily exercise is necessary to every animal at all times of the year. Even during the coldest part of winter, animals should be exercised or turned out for part of the day.

Exercise tones up flabby muscles, gets the blood circulating, and energizes animals. It also helps to keep them from putting on unhealthy weight.

Grooming

Except for horses, most stock animals are not groomed regularly, but only for show purposes. Nevertheless, all livestock benefits from grooming.

It helps to keep them clean, stimulates blood circulation, and cuts down the chance of skin disease. Also, during grooming, a stockman may see cuts and bruises that should be cared for.

Clean, well-groomed animals are more comfortable and less likely to spread infections or parasites to other animals.

Careers in Livestock Production

Because plants and livestock are the base for most of our food supply, you could hardly choose a more important career than farming or ranching. Without the farmers and other workers who produce our food and fiber, the world's soaring population could not exist.

The farmer is the most vital link in the chain of growing, processing, transporting, and marketing of food and fibers. The whole chain is called agribusiness, and it is the nation's largest industry.

Here we are concerned with livestock producers, not with the processers, movers, and marketers of food and fiber. What is the outlook for careers in livestock production?

The answer has two parts. The outlook is great—but for a shrinking number of people actually on farms and ranches. The number of farmers and other on-farm workers has been decreasing for some years, although the rate of decline appears to be leveling off.

The reason is simple. Each on-farm worker is many times more productive than in years past. A hundred years ago a farmer produced enough food and fiber for himself and four other people. Today he produces enough for more than 45 others.

And so, while our overall farm and ranch production has grown even faster than the world's population, the need for farm labor has dropped steadily. Advances in scientific methods of production and in transportation and marketing systems have tended to make the big farm more efficient than the small. The need for complex management and expensive machinery has also contributed to the trend to larger farm and ranch operations.

Because of these trends, only one farm boy in five becomes a farmer. But he can look forward to an exciting, satisfying, and well-paying career. Of the 80 percent of farm boys who do not become farmers, many go into other phases of agribusiness and find good careers, too.

There are many types of livestock - producing farmers and ranchers. Some specialize in one kind of stock—horses, beef cattle, dairy cattle, sheep, goats, hogs, or poultry. Others may have smaller herds or flocks of two or more kinds of animals.

Most of these farmers and ranchers grow crops as well as livestock; a large majority grow nearly all the grains and forage needed by their stock. So if you are thinking about a career as a stockman, you will want to earn the Plant Science merit badge, too.

Livestock Farm Employees

Years ago most farms were family operations. The farmer, his wife, and their children were able to handle most of the necessary work themselves. They may have had help from neighbors during planting and harvest, but they were largely self-sufficient. This is still true on many small farms.

But with the trend toward fewer but bigger farms and ranches, there is a greater need for hired employees. So opportunities are available for skilled farm workers.

Nearly all farms of any size today need farm hands or laborers. Big cattle ranches require cowboys to tend the stock, and other kinds of livestock farms also need hands. On a small stock farm worked by only the farmer and one or two other men, the hands may have a wide variety of tasks.

Large farms and ranches are often owned by commercial companies or by individuals who do not live on the farm. A skilled farmer is hired to manage the farm. Depending on the type, he might be called a farm manager, foreman, cattleman, dairyman, dairy herdsman, poultryman, hatchery manager, or swineherdsman. He does everything a self-employed farmer would do, but he is a paid employee.

There are also on-farm jobs for workers with special skills. Here are examples:

Animal Groom. His job is to keep animals in good condition for showing.

Cattle Dehorner. A person who removes horns or prevents them from growing by using electric dehorners or by applying chemicals on the buttons. Dehorned cattle are less dangerous and more easily managed.

Chick Sexer. He is a hatchery employee who separates chicks by sex.
Egg-room Foreman. A special hatchery employee who sorts and trays eggs before hatching. He also supervises workers who inspect eggs.

Milking Operator. Milks cows twice daily in automated milking parlor. He also keeps records of milk production and keeps cows healthy.

Horseshoer or Farrier. The village smithy is long gone, but there is still a need for skilled horseshoers. Many work on ranches and at race tracks.

Horse Trainer. A specialized worker who trains young horses for pleasure riding or racing.

Stableman. On a horse farm, he grooms, feeds, and tends the stock.

Custom or Contract Work

In major farm areas, some workers earn part of their living by going from farm to farm on contract. They provide services that cannot be done as economically (or perhaps as skillfully) by the farmer or his workers.

One example is the sheep shearer. His is a seasonal job, lasting about 2 months during the spring and early summer. Usually he carries his own equipment as he moves from farm to farm.

Preparing for a Career

As farmwork has become more scientific and more mechanized, the need for more education and special training has increased. Today's farmer and rancher must have considerable skill in many fields.

He must be an accountant, mechanic, and merchandiser, as well as a planter and livestock raiser. He must be familiar with crop science, nutrition needs of animals, and machinery repair. His employees, too, must have skills and knowledge beyond that required to follow a horse-drawn plow. Most farm employees, in fact, are skilled, or at least semiskilled workers.

There are no definite educational qualifications for on-farm work. But there is no question that a high-school diploma is an asset because it shows proficiency in some areas that are essential in modern farming. Many farmers and ranchers today have college degrees in agriculture. Others take special courses through agricultural colleges and in vocational education programs.

On-farm experience is, of course, essential for young men whose career goal is livestock production. Farm boys get it as they grow up. But nonfarm boys can get valuable agriculture courses in high school, through 4-H clubs and Future Farmers of America (FFA), and by actual work on a farm.

Any ambitious young man who likes outdoor work and who finds satisfaction in making things grow should consider a career in livestock production.

Resources for Your Specialty

Recommended by the American Library Association's Advisory Committee to Scouting and the U.S. Department of Agriculture

Because space is limited in this booklet, it is not possible to give detailed information on each of the livestock options for require ment 6. Many resources are available to you for details you will need.

Check the following:

- Experienced producers of your livestock choice.
- Cooperative extension office, sometimes called county extension office. This is home base for your county agent, whose job is to counsel farmers and ranchers and give them information about scientific advances in agriculture. If you don't know where your county extension office is, look in the phone book under "U.S. Government," your state, or your county.
- Vocational agriculture teachers. There are nearly 9,000 vocational agriculture programs with 13,000 teachers in high schools across the country. Unless you live in a major metropolitan area, one of those schools is probably within your reach.
- Future Farmers of America chapter. The FFA is a national organization of students who are aiming for careers in agriculture and agribusiness.
- 4-H clubs.
- School and public libraries.
- Livestock dealers and salesmen.

If possible, visit the county extension office before starting on requirement 6. Useful material should be found there. For example, 4-H manuals prepared by state 4-H clubs and FFA publications probably will be on file for use.

General Materials About Animals

4-H BULLETINS
Horse Science
Horses and Horsemanship

U.S DEPARTMENT OF AGRICULTURE BULLETINS
Raising Livestock on Small Farms, F 2224
Farm Poultry Management, F 2197
Outdoor Safety Tips, PA 887

OTHER BULLETINS
Exploring Careers in Modern Agriculture, Pennsylvania State University, Department of Agricultural Education, 102 Armsby, University Park, Pa. 16802
Digestion in Animals, VAS 1026, University of Illinois, Vocational Agriculture Service (VAS), 434 Mumford Hall, Urbana, Ill. 61801
Improving Animals Through Breeding, VAS 1009, Illinois VAS, address above
Livestock Breeding, Ohio State University, Extension Office of Information, 2120 Fyfe Road,

Columbus, Ohio 43210

BOOKS

Briggs, Hilton, *Modern Breeds of Livestock*. 1958. Macmillan

Bundy, C.E., and Diggins, R.V., *Livestock and Poultry Production*. 1968. Prentice-Hall

Dent, A.A., and Davis, P.D., *Animals That Changed the World*. 1968. Macmillan

Fenton, Carroll L., and Kitchen, Herminie D., *Animals That Help Us*. 1959. E.M. Hale & Co., Eau Claire, Wis. 54701

Hoover, Norman K., *Handbook of Agricultural Occupations*. 1969. Interstate Printers and Publishers, Danville, Ill. 61832

McCoy, Joseph J., *Animal Servants of Man*. 1963. Lothrop, Lee & Shepard, West Caldwell, N.J. 07006

Parker, Bertha M., *Domesticated Animals*. Harper and Row

Horses

4-H BULLETINS

Horse Science
Horses and Horsemanship

U.S DEPARTMENT OF AGRICULTURE BULLETINS

Portable Stable for a Horse, plan No. 6082, M 1188

Horse Bots: How To Control Them, L 450

African Horsesickness—an Old Disease—a New Menace, PA 596

OTHER BULLETINS

Horses—Complete Management, Albers Milling Co., 800 West 47th St., Kansas City, Mo. 64112

Student's Study Guide for Horse Farm Employees, University of Kentucky, Department of Vocational Education, Lexington, Ky. 40500

BOOKS

Anderson, Clarence W., *Heads Up, Heels Down*. 1944. Macmillan

Duggan, Moira, *Horses*. 1972. Western Publishing Co.

Ensminger, M.E., *Horses and Horsemanship*. 1969. Interstate Printers and Publishers, Danville, Ill. 61832

Gorman, John R., *The Western Horse*. 1967. Interstate Printers and Publishers

Johnson, Pat, *Horse Talk*. 1967. Funk & Wagnalls

McMillan, George, *Golden Book of Horses*. 1968. Western Publishing Co.

Nissen, Jasper, *Young Horseman's Guide*. A.S. Barnes

Self, Margaret C., *Complete Book of Horses and Ponies*. 1963. McGraw-Hill

Sutton, Felix, *Horses of America*. 1964. Putnam

Ulmer, D.E., and Juergenson, E.M., *Approved Practices in Raising and Handling Horses*. 1974. Interstate Printers and Publishers

Dairy Cattle

U.S. DEPARTMENT OF AGRICULTURE BULLETINS

Cattle Lice: How To Control Them, L 456

Fescue Foot in Cattle—What To Do About It, L 546

Rinderpest...a Highly Contagious Virus Disease of Cattle, PA 944

OTHER BULLETINS

Care of the Dry and Fresh Cow, PM 249, Iowa State University, Cooperative Extension Service, Public Distribution Center, Printing and Publishing Building, Ames, Iowa 50010

Feeding for Milk Production, PM 282, ISU Extension Service, address above

Feeding the Dairy Calf, ISU Extension Service, address above

Dairy Calf Diseases, ISU Extension Service, address above

Calf-Growing Program, Land O' Lakes Felco, 2927 8th Ave. South, Fort Dodge, Iowa 50511

Dairy Cattle Breeds, VAS 1046, University of Illinois Vocational Agriculture Service (VAS), 434 Mumford Hall, Urbana, Ill. 61801

Raising Dairy Calves, VAS 1021, Illinois VAS, address above

Basic Dairy Herd Health, Wisconsin Department of Public Instruction, Bureau of Career and Manpower Development, Madison, Wis. 53702

Quality Milk Production, Pennsylvania State University, Department of Agricultural Education, University Park, Pa. 16802

Guernsey Fitting and Salesmanship, The American Guernsey Cattle Club, Peterborough, N.H. 03458

How To Judge Guernseys, The American Guernsey Cattle Club, address above

Junior Holstein Heifer Project, Holstein-Friesian Association of America, Box 808, Brattleboro, Vt. 05301

Judging Registered Holsteins, Holstein-Friesian Association of America, address above

Dairy Cattle Judging Made Easy, M-4-1, Animal Science Department, Cornell University, Ithaca, N.Y. 14850

Hoard's Dairymen Feed Guide, 64 pages, Hoard's Dairymen, Fort Atkinson, Wis. 53538

Hoard's Dairymen—Herd Health Guide, Hoard's Dairymen, address above

An Introduction to Brown Swiss, The Brown Swiss Cattle Breeders' Association, Box 1038, Beloit, Wis. 53511

Clipping Is a Big Part of Grooming, The Brown Swiss Cattle Breeders' Association, address above

Try Registered Ayrshires, Ayrshire Breeders' Association, Brandon, Vt. 05733

BOOKS

Ensminger, M.E., *Beef Cattle Science*. 1968. Interstate Printers and Publishers, Danville, Ill. 61832

Foley, R.C., Bath, D.L., Dickinson, F.N., and Lucke, H.A., *Dairy Cattle — Principles, Practices, Problems, and Profits*. 1972. Lea and Febiger, Philadelphia, Pa.

Juergenson, E.M., and Mortenson, W.P., *Approved Practices in*

Dairying. 1972. Interstate Printers and Publishers

Schmidt, G.H., and Van Vleck, L.D., *Principles of Dairy Science.* 1974. W.H. Freeman and Co., San Francisco, Calif.

Beef Cattle

U.S. DEPARTMENT OF AGRICULTURE BULLETINS

Beef Cattle: Dehorning, Castrating, Branding, and Marking, F 2141

Corral Layout...and Equipment for Beef Cattle, plan No. 6106, M 1228

The Farm Beef Herd, F 2126

Finishing Beef Cattle, F 2196

Six Corrals for Beef Cattle, plan No. 5835, M 776

USDA Yield Grades for Beef, MB 45

OTHER BULLETINS

Managing the Beef Breeding Herd, University of Illinois, Vocational Agriculture Service (VAS), 434 Mumford Hall, Urbana, Ill. 61801

Beef Production Guide, Land O' Lakes Felco, 2827 8th Ave. South, Fort Dodge, Iowa 50511

Approved Practices for Beef, Illinois VAS, address above

Star of Your Future, American Angus Association, 3201 Frederick Boulevard, St. Joseph, Mo. 64501

BOOKS

Arnold, Oren, *Story of Cattle Ranching.* 1968. Harvey House, Irvington, N.J. 10533

Ensminger, M.E., *Beef Cattle Science.* 1968. Interstate Printers and Publishers, Danville, Ill. 61832

Juergenson, E.M., *Approved Practices in Beef Cattle Production.* 1973. Interstate Printers and Publishers

Sheep

U.S. DEPARTMENT OF AGRICULTURE BULLETINS

Docking, Castrating, and Ear-Tagging Lambs, M 1148

Housing and Equipment for Sheep, F 2242

OTHER BULLETINS

Twelve Keys to Profits in Lamb Production, Iowa State University, Cooperative Extension Service, Ames, Iowa 50010

Applied Sheep Nutrition, PM 419, ISU Extension, address above

Selecting and Purchasing Sheep, VAS 1031, University of Illinois, Vocational Agriculture Service (VAS), 434 Mumford Hall, Urbana, Ill. 61801

Feeding Lambs, Illinois VAS, address above

The Sheep Enterprise, VAS 1031, Illinois VAS, address above

BOOKS

Ensminger, M.E., *Sheep and Wool Science.* 1970. Interstate Printers and Publishers, Danville, Ill. 61832

Juergenson, E.M., *Approved Practices in Sheep Production.* 1973. Interstate Printers and Publishers

Hogs

U.S. DEPARTMENT OF AGRICULTURE BULLETINS

Breeds of Swine, F 1263
Hog Castration, L 473
The Meat-Type Hog, L 429

OTHER BULLETINS

Life Cycle Swine Nutrition, PM 489, Iowa State University, Cooperative Extension Service, Ames, Iowa 50010

Swine Production Guide, Land O' Lakes Felco, 2827 8th Ave. South, Fort Dodge, Iowa 50511

The Swine Enterprise, VAS 1029, University of Illinois, Vocational Agriculture Service (VAS), 434 Mumford Hall, Urbana, Ill. 61801

Swine Nutrition, 536, 537, Michigan State University, Cooperative Extension Service, East Lansing, Mich. 48823

BOOKS

Baker, J.K., and Juergenson, E.M., *Approved Practices in Swine Production.* 1971. Interstate Printers and Publishers, Danville, Ill. 61832

Bundy, C.E., and Diggins, R.V., *Swine Production.* 1970. Prentice-Hall

Ensminger, M.E., *Swine Science.* 1970. Interstate Printers and Publishers

Poultry

U.S. DEPARTMENT OF AGRICULTURE BULLETINS

Farm Poultry Management, F 2197
Raising Ducks, F 2215
Raising Geese, F 2251
Raising Guinea Fowl, L 519

OTHER BULLETINS

Feeding Replacement Pullets and Laying Hens, PM 354, Iowa State University, Cooperative Extension Service, Ames, Iowa 50010

Poultry Industry Project, PM 418, ISU Extension Service, address above

BOOKS

Biddle, George, and Juergenson, E.M., *Approved Practices in Poultry Production.* 1963. Interstate Printers and Publishers, Danville, Ill. 61832

Bundy, C.E., and Diggins, R.V., *Livestock and Poultry Production.* 1968. Prentice-Hall

Darling, Louis, *Chickens and How To Raise Them,* 1955. Morrow

Ensminger, M.E., *Poultry Science.* Interstate Printers and Publishers

ACKNOWLEDGMENTS

This pamphlet was prepared under the supervision of the following committee members and their associates: R.J. Hildreth, managing director, Farm Foundation; Dr. Kemp L. Swiney, program leader, 4-H—USDA; and H.N. Hunsicker, national adviser, Future Farmers of America, Department of Health, Education and Welfare.

Technical assistance and illustrations were provided by Dr. Charles E. Hess, dean of Cook College, Rutgers University, and his staff; the Interstate Printers and Publishers, Danville, Ill.; the U.S. Department of Agriculture; the Agriservices Foundation; and the American Shetland Pony Club.